GOD'S STORY

Text copyright © 1997 by Jan Mark
Illustrations copyright © 1997 by David Parkins

First U.S. edition 1998

Library of Congress Cataloging-in-Publication Data

Mark, Jan.
God's story / retold by Jan Mark ; illustrated by David Parkins.
— 1st U.S. ed.
p. cm.
Summary: An illustrated retelling of stories from the Old Testament, including
"The First Seven Days," "The Cities on the Plain," and "The Plagues and the Passover."
ISBN 0-7636-0376-7
1. Bible stories, English — O.T. [1. Bible stories — O.T.]
I. Parkins, David, ill. II. Title.
BS551.2.M34 1998
221.9'505 — dc21 97-18558

2 4 6 8 10 9 7 5 3 1

Printed in Singapore

This book was typeset in Truesdell.
The pictures were done in white gouache and
black ink, and were digitally colored.

Candlewick Press
2067 Massachusetts Avenue
Cambridge, Massachusetts 02140

GOD'S STORY

Jan Mark

illustrated by David Parkins

CANDLEWICK PRESS
CAMBRIDGE, MASSACHUSETTS

For Kathy Lowinger
J. M.

For Harriet Alice —
my most important contribution to the story
D. P.

Contents

Introduction	6
The First Seven Days	11
Noah's Box	27
The Jewel in the Sand	39
The Cities on the Plain	53
Sons and Brothers	67
The Dreamer in Egypt	81
The Plagues and the Passover	95
The Gift of Torah	109
The Battle for Canaan	123
Saul and David	137
Solomon and After	151
The Second Promise	167

Introduction

THE OLD TESTAMENT is full of stories. Even people who never open a Bible know the stories: Adam and Eve in the Garden of Eden; Cain and Abel; Joseph and his brothers; Moses and the Ten Commandments. But it is also a complete story in itself, and because it is not customary, or very rewarding, to read the Old Testament straight through, like a novel, readers do not always notice that the tales about people are essential parts of this much longer story. It tells how God made the universe and then, when he had finished it, he created mankind to enjoy all the other things that he had made, only to discover that no matter how much he loved his humans they could rarely be bothered to remember him, much less worship him or even thank him. Because they could not see God, they preferred to make idols and worship *them*, to thank them when things went well and to ask for their help in times of trouble. God was frequently on the point of giving up on his disappointing creatures and wiping them out before they ruined everything else that he had made, but at last he thought he could see a solution to the problem. He chose one man, Abraham, who believed in God and not in idols, and promised that his descendants should be God's own people if they in their turn would promise to worship him as their one and only God.

Abraham kept his side of the bargain, but it was impossible to rely on the people who came after him; and the story—whether you believe it or not—is of the struggle between God and the people he had chosen. The people gave up over and over again but God never did—quite.

That is the story told in this book, but it is not exactly the story as you will find it in the Old Testament, whichever version or translation you use. It is impossible to read the Old Testament without asking questions that are not answered: Why did God accept Abel's sacrifice and not Cain's? Why ask for sacrifices at all? Why did God choose Abraham to be the father of the chosen people—and then tell him to kill his own son? Why did Jacob wrestle with an angel? Why was Moses forbidden to enter the Promised

7

Land? And where, you might ask, is Satan, a figure of great power and fear to Muslims and Christians?

There are considerable differences between the beliefs of Jews, Muslims, and Christians, but originally they all came from the same part of the world, and they share the same stories. Christians call the Old Testament the first part of their Bible. For Jews it is the only part. Muslims do not use the Bible at all—the book of Islam is the Koran—but many of the people and stories that appear in the Koran are also found in the Old Testament. The account of man's creation appears in both books, and it is in the Koran that we read of the uncooperative angel who was thrown out of heaven for refusing to bow down to Adam, not, as many people think, for refusing to bow down to God. Eventually he became known as Satan, then the Devil, God's great adversary. In this book you will find that he is called Samael, and he is never permitted to be much more than a nuisance.

Two thousand years ago a succession of Jewish scholars called rabbis began to discuss the Torah, the first five books of the Old Testament. Since these books were the word of God, they could not be altered, but they had originally been given to a primitive, nomadic people. Now these people lived in cities under military occupation by a foreign power. The questions they had to ask were urgent and important, so the rabbis set out to debate *every word* of the Torah so that in the future the answers would be there for anyone who needed them. To make their ideas clear they told little stories so that people would understand the more difficult points. Christians who see a story like this told by Jesus in the New Testament call it a parable. Jews call it a Midrash, which is what Jesus, himself a Jew, would have called it. Collected together they are known as the *Midrash Rabbah* — the Great Midrash — and much of this book is taken from it.

It ends at the point where serious disputes were arising from the fact that, whereas previously, different religions worshipped different gods, there were now three religions developing with the same god, all three at odds about the ways in which he should be worshipped and his laws obeyed. People still fight to the death about this, so it might be good to stop here with the words of one of the first great rabbis, Hillel, who said, "Do nothing to other people that you would not want them to do to you. That is the whole Law. The rest is commentary." He was referring to the Law of Moses, which contains six hundred and thirteen commandments, but imagine what the world would be like if all mankind took his advice, whatever their religion. They are perhaps the wisest words ever spoken.

The First Seven Days

IN THE BEGINNING GOD
created the dark, and in
that darkness he made
heaven and earth, and
did not see what he was
making. So God said:
Let there be light.
And there was light.

God looked at what he had made. The heaven and the earth were shapeless and confused, one with the other, land and water and air. But it was a beginning and it was good. God called the light Day and the darkness he called Night, and when light had followed darkness the first day was over.

Then dark followed light and day followed night. God made the sky and said: *Its name is Heaven.* Then he divided the water between heaven and earth and the water in heaven was rain. And from the fiery light he made angels, and on the second day, God was no longer alone.

13

On the third day God called
together all the waters under heaven and
let the dry land appear. He named the dry
land Earth and the water he named Sea.
And on that day also he made all green
things that grow: the first blade of grass,
the first great tree. And as the third day
ended God looked at what he had made
and he knew that it was good.

And God took the light that was all around and made from it the sun, the moon, the stars. He set them like lamps in heaven to shine upon earth: the sun by day, the moon and stars by night. All this was done on the fourth day, and it was good.

15

And in the seas God made great whales and little fish. He made creatures with wings to live in the sky. Then he blessed them all and sent them away to swim and fly. That was the fifth day, and it was good.

On the sixth day God made all the creatures that were to live upon the dry land, and when he had finished he knew that there was still one thing more to be done, so he said to the angels: *Now I shall make a man and a woman, and everything else that I have made will be for them and for their children, evermore, until the last day of time.*

17

And the angels said, "What for? What need is there for man and woman? No good will come of it."

But while they argued, God took dust from the four corners of the earth and made a man and a woman, and breathed life into them. Then he said to the angels: *It is too late to argue. Man and woman are made. His name is Adam. Her name is Eve. Bow down before them.*

The angels said again, "No good will come of this. The children of that man and that woman will shed blood and kill each other."

God said: *You did not ask me why I made heaven and earth, and beasts and cattle and birds and fish. What use is a place full of good things if there are no guests to enjoy them? All things have been made for a reason, as you will see, even fleas and flies and scorpions. But I love my man and my woman the most, so I have made them in my image, to look like me. Still I have made them last of all, so that they may not be proud, for even the gnat was made before they were. Now, bow down.*

But the angels had been made first, and

they were proud. At last they bowed down, all except one, the proudest of all, and his name was Samael, who spread his twelve great wings and said, "You made me from fiery light. Should I bow down before a thing made of dust?"

God said: *You shall.*

Samael said, "I shall not."

God said: *Then out of my sight shall you go, out of heaven.*

And Samael said, "Very well, but for all time to come I shall lie in wait for your little man of dust, and if he does not obey you, then he shall obey me."

And God said: *Very well. But remember this: Fire or dust, I made you both. You may tell man that you are my equal, but we know that you are lying, you and I, and so will he, on the last day of time.*

Then Samael turned and dropped like a falling star from heaven, and evil came down to earth with him.

But God took the new man and the new woman and set them in a garden upon the new earth. And he said to them: *All this is yours. It is Paradise. Be happy, love one another, have children. Enjoy all that I have given you, except one thing only. In the middle of this garden grows a tree that you must not touch. If you eat the fruit from that tree, you will die. Do you understand?*

Adam looked all around. He saw the trees, the fruit, the flowers, and the grass beneath his feet. He saw the birds in the air and the fish in the waters, the beasts and the cattle and all the creeping things that God had made. And Adam said, "What is that? What is this? What are these?"

God said: *Whatever you call them, those are their names.*

And that was the sixth day. God left Adam and Eve in the garden with all the living things, calling out their names.

This was the end of God's making, when the first star appeared on the evening of the sixth day. On the seventh day, he rested.

20

Now, there was one creature upon earth that Adam named Serpent.

The serpent strolled in the garden on its long legs, and it saw the woman, Eve, looking at the tree that God had said she must not touch. The serpent was a clever beast, and curious, and envious. Perhaps the fallen angel, Samael, whispered in its ear, who knows? But the serpent came up to the woman and said, "What are you waiting for? God has said you may eat all the fruit in the garden. That is the finest fruit of all. Eat it."

The woman said, "Not that fruit."

The serpent said, "Then why is it there?"

The woman said, "I do not know. But God says that if we eat that fruit we shall die."

21

"Not so," said the serpent, as it stood by the woman. "If you eat that fruit you will not die. But God is jealous. He means to keep all knowledge to himself. If you eat that fruit you will be like God, knowing everything."

And then you will tell *me* everything, the serpent thought.

The woman thought, Why not? And she called to Adam, "Hear what the serpent says. If we eat this fruit we shall not die, but we shall be like God, knowing everything." Then she picked the fruit and bit into it and gave it to Adam, and he bit into it. And they looked at each other.

They were not like God. They did not know everything. But they knew that they were naked and ashamed and cold and afraid.

And as day turned to evening they heard God walking in his garden among all that he had made, and they wrapped themselves in leaves, and hid. And God called out: *Adam, where are you? I see all the birds and the fish and the beasts and the cattle and creeping things that I have made, but where are my man and my woman?*

23

Adam and Eve crept out of the trees and stood before God all wrapped in leaves. Adam said, "I was afraid when I heard your voice, for I knew that I was naked."

And God said: *Who told you that?* But he knew what had happened. *I told you not to eat the fruit of one tree and you have eaten it.*

And Adam said, "That woman you made, she told me to eat it."

Oh, it's my fault, is it? said God. And he said to the woman: *What have you done, and why?*

And the woman said, "The serpent told me to."

Then God saw that all the good things he had made were beginning to go wrong, and that what had been perfect was spoiled. He said to the serpent: *Down on your belly and stay there. You and your kind shall walk on your bellies forever, and the woman and her children will crush you when they can.*

Then the serpent slipped out of its skin and slithered away, and it is slithering still.

To Adam and Eve God said: *Here in my*

garden you would have lived forever and been happy. But now you must go out into the world to work and suffer, and at the end of your lives—for now your lives will end—you will go back into the dust of the earth, for from the dust of the earth I created you.

Then he made them clothes of the serpent's skin, to cover and warm themselves, and sent them away, out of the garden that was Paradise, to live as best they could.

And at the edge of the garden he set cherubim, fiery angels with a blazing sword, so that man and woman could never come back to the garden, ever again. In six days he had made everything perfect, and on the seventh day it was spoiled.

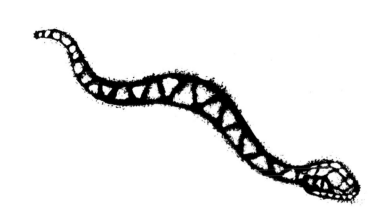

Noah's Box

So God and his angels were in heaven, and the man and the woman were alone on earth, knowing too much, but not enough. For they had been given everything, and had lost it all, and now they had to make their own way, to work and to suffer.

They worked together and suffered together and up in heaven God watched. They had disbelieved him and disobeyed him, but they were his. He had made them. He still loved them.

They worked together and lived together and after a time the woman, Eve, gave birth to twins. The girl she named Luluwa, the boy she named Cain.

Not long after they had more children, a son, Abel, and his twin sisters.

Now Cain grew up and dug in the ground and planted seeds. He grew corn and fruit and vegetables, and at harvest time Adam said to his son Cain, the farmer, "Choose the best of the crop and offer it to God. He made all things to grow and a present will please him."

Abel too had grown up. He went about the hills and fields and cared for the white woolly beasts that Adam had called sheep, long ago on the sixth day of the world. When all the flock was gathered together, Adam said to his son Abel, the shepherd, "Choose the best of the flock and offer them to God. He made all things to grow and a gift will please him."

So Cain took fruit and vegetables and corn and laid them out where God would see them. Abel brought his finest and fattest sheep with their lambs, so that God would see that he was grateful for his good fortune.

God leaned down from heaven to look at his presents. He saw that Cain had brought him fine fruit and vegetables and ears of corn, but none of it was better than the food Cain ate himself. Abel had chosen the very best of his flock as a gift for God. So God let them know that Abel's was the better gift, the one that pleased him most.

And when Cain knew what God thought he scowled with rage, and God said: *Cain, Cain, what is the matter? Why are you angry? Why do you scowl?*

And God thought, Now is the moment to teach him better ways. And God said: *If you do well, then I shall be pleased. But remember, Samael is always lying in wait to trap you. He told me so himself. But there is no need to be trapped. You can do well if you try.*

But Cain was not listening, or he did not understand, who knows? He went out into the field with Abel his brother, saying, "Why should God be pleased with you and not with me? Why does he praise your gift and not mine?"

29

And then he shouted, and then he raised his fist. He struck Abel his brother and Abel fell down dead. Cain was afraid and did not understand. He knew that he had done a bad thing, but he did not know what it was. No one had ever died before. This was the first death.

But God was watching. He knew what had happened. He called out: *Cain? Cain? Where is Abel, your brother?*

And Cain said, "How should I know? Am I supposed to watch over him every minute?" And he was even more afraid.

God said: *Oh, Cain, what have you done? I know all that happens on this earth that I have made. I know what you do and what you think, and I know that even now your brother's blood is soaking into the earth. Rain from heaven should water the earth, not the blood of your brother. Things will never grow so well for you again. And now you must go away, for I cannot keep you here.*

At last Cain understood the dreadful thing that he had done, and he cried to God, "Is my sin too great to be forgiven? If you drive me

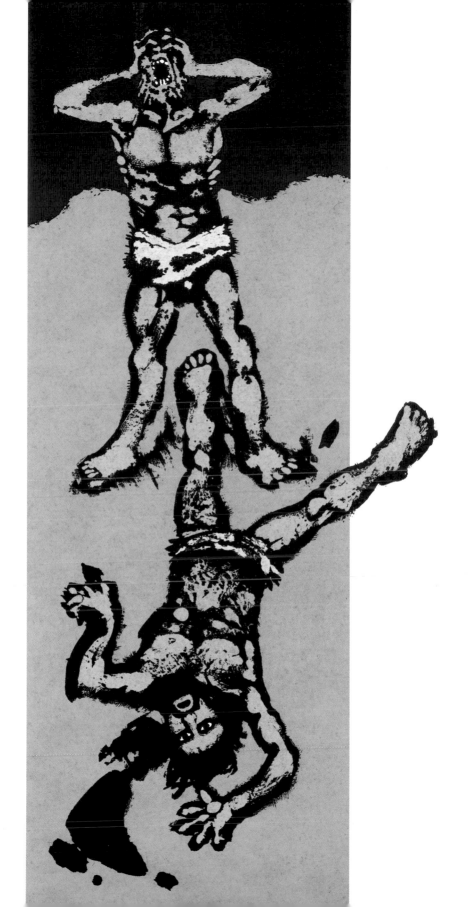

away I shall wander the earth and no one will help me. People will know what I have done, and kill me."

God thought, This is only the third person upon earth. Already he has killed his brother and is afraid that other men will kill him. He is right and the angels were right. Men kill one another.

So God leaned down and touched the face of Cain and said: *Have no fear, I have marked you out with the first letter of my own name. No one will kill you or they will have me to reckon with. Now go.*

And Cain turned and walked away, away from God, who watched him go.

32

Now, meanwhile, Adam and Eve had another son, named Seth, and other sons and other daughters. One of these became the wife of Cain and they too had sons and daughters. Now there were people spreading out all over the earth, and God watched them and hoped that things might turn out well after all.

For Cain and his wife had a son called Enoch. And that son had a son, and so did that son after him; more and more people spreading out over the earth. And wherever there were men and women, there too was Samael, lying in wait. And Seth, the third son of Adam and Eve, had children of his own, and they in their turn had children, and every day there were more people.

And at last there was born a man called Noah, and he was born just in time. For God was looking down on the world, and he saw the children of the man and woman that he had made, and all that he saw was bad. He remembered the perfect world that he had made and he saw what man had done to it, and he wished that he had never made man in the first place.

33

And he said to himself: *It is spoiled, it is ruined, and I am forgotten, I who made it. I am going to destroy it before it gets any worse. I am going to destroy everything in it, men and beasts and cattle and fish and birds. The more I look at what has happened, the more I wish I had never begun.*

And he lifted his hand to destroy the earth that he had made and every living thing in it, on the land, in the sea, in the air; and then he looked down and saw Noah. And stopped.

Now, although he lived in evil times, Noah was not an evil man. And God thought, This one may be worth keeping, for the sake of those who come after him.

So down he went again and said to Noah: *Enough is enough. I made a perfect world and men have so wrecked it that I cannot bear to see what they have done. I am going to destroy it and everything in it, but for your sake I will give mankind one last chance. Listen carefully, Noah, and do exactly as I tell you.*

34

Noah listened, and he could scarcely credit what he was hearing. *I want you,* said God, *to make a very large box.*

"I hear you, Lord," Noah said.

With rooms in it.

"A box with *rooms?*"

On three storys, God said. *This box is to be three hundred cubits long, and fifty wide, and thirty cubits high.*

Noah looked at his forearm, which was one cubit long, and began to understand what he was being told to do.

And God said: *When it is made and caulked with pitch, inside and out, I shall open the heavens above and the springs below and flood the earth from end to end, and every living thing on it will die. But Noah,* said God, *do as I say now, and I will spare you. When the box is ready, go into it with your wife, and your sons and their wives too. And in that box that you will make, take animals also: two of each, male and female, except for the ones that you can eat. You may take fourteen each of those, birds and cattle.*

35

And Noah said, "Lord, must I go out and find them all?"

And God said: *No, I will send them to you, for you will be busy enough. See those trees? Take an ax. Start work.*

So Noah began to make the great box. It took him five years and people thought he was mad. But all the while that he was building the box, from far and wide the animals came, one by one and seven by seven, for the angels were sent by God to round them up.

And when all was ready, Noah called to the animals and they entered the box one by one and seven by seven, except for the worm Shamir. For there is only ever one Shamir, and alone it went into the box, for God knew that one day it would be needed.

Then Noah's family went inside, and Noah last of all, into the fearsome dark, and God closed the box, saying: *Noah, there was once a king who shut up his friend in prison, even as you are shut into this box. And the friend was afraid, for he did not know that the king was about to destroy* the city, and had locked him away to save him. *Trust me, Noah*, said God.

Then the rain began to fall, and water gushed up from beneath the ground, and God watched every living thing die that he had made. For forty days and forty nights there seemed no end to the rain, and the water covered the face of the earth.

But the box floated.

The Jewel in the Sand

FOR A HUNDRED DAYS and fifty more, the rain fell and the springs gushed, until all the water that ever was, lay upon the face of the earth, and every living breathing thing that God had made to live upon land, perished.

But the great box floated still, and in the darkness, cold and airless, Noah lived on with his wife and his sons and their wives, and the animals that God had saved.

And God, in heaven, remembered Noah and the promise that he had made to him, and at the end of one hundred and fifty days he stopped the springs and closed the windows of heaven, and the waters began to fall away until mountaintops appeared. And on a mountain slope the great box came to rest at last.

But Noah was still afraid and waited forty days more until he dared to look out, and then he saw that the waters were still all around him, so he sent out a raven to see if there was yet any dry land.

"Why send me?" said the raven, and spread its wings to coast to and fro upon the wind. It had no need of land.

And after the raven Noah sent a dove, but she found no place to perch and returned to Noah.

So he waited seven days and sent out the dove again, and when she came back she carried a green leaf in her beak, and Noah knew that life was returning to earth, and things were growing again.

But Noah waited. God had shut him up in the box and only God could set him free. At last, when all the water had vanished and the earth was dry again, God called to Noah and said: *Now you may go, you and your wife and your sons and their wives, and take with you all the living things that you and I have saved. This is a new beginning, a second chance, said God. All that went wrong before has been wiped out. Start again.*

So Noah and his family left the box, and all the animals with them that God and Noah had saved. God watched them go and said to himself: *There is no use in punishing man for the*

41

bad things that he does, for mankind will always do bad things. There is no help for it. Better to wait till the last day of time to settle accounts. Until that day all shall be as I meant it to be. Summer shall follow winter, harvest shall follow seedtime, day shall follow night.

And to Noah God said, as he had said to Adam: All this is yours. Enjoy what I have given you. Be happy. Have children. Live at peace. I make you a promise that never again will I send a flood to destroy the earth and everything in it. Here is a sign to prove it.

And as the sun shone for the first time since the rain began to fall, God drew a circle of lights about the earth. Noah and his family, where they stood, saw the half of it and thought that it looked like an archer's bow, bent toward heaven. And ever after, when men saw it in the sky, they knew it for a sign that rain was over and ended, and never again would water cover the earth. That was the promise that God made, and God kept his promise.

But the sons of Noah — Japhet and Ham and Shem — had promised nothing. They and their wives had sons and daughters, and they in their turn had sons and daughters, generation after generation, and once again people spread out over the earth.

And God watched from heaven to see what would happen this time. And he saw the promise was forgotten.

For men remembered the flood, in the days of their ancestors, but they forgot who had sent it, and why.

They said to one another, "From time to time, the heavens are shaken and break open. This is dangerous. It lets the water through. Let us build a great tower to steady the sky. And if God does not like it, then we will set a statue on top with a sword in its hand to show that we dare to disobey him."

So they set to and made many bricks, for they reckoned that this tower must be seven miles high.

43

And God thought, *Now* what are they doing? And he went down to find out.

And he saw all the people working together to build the tower, all speaking the same language, all working as one.

God thought, These people are working together like brothers, I cannot fault them for that. But again they have forgotten me, I who made them. They understand one another too well. *Let us go down*, he said to the angels, *and put a stop to this.*

And with men's own tongues he put a stop to it. For one man said to another, "Bring me water," and the other brought him clay, for he did not understand what he was asked, and they fought each other. A man said to his fellow, "Bring me an ax," and the fellow brought him a spade, and they fought.

And so they all fell out, and the building stopped. The tower tumbled and the workers each went his own way, for now they all spoke different words, and so they do, to this very day.

And God, back in heaven, waited for men to remember him, but they did not, except for one.

There was a man called Terah, who made idols, gods of wood and clay and stone. God watched men buy the idols that Terah made. They took them home and set them up and worshipped the idols instead of God, for they did not trust in a god they could not see.

But one day Terah was called away and left his son Abram to mind the shop. In came a man to buy an idol, and Abram said to him, "Do you believe that this is a god?" And the man said, "Yes."

Abram said, "How old are you?"

And the man said, "I have been on earth for fifty years."

And Abram thought, How can a man who has been on earth for fifty years worship a thing that has been on earth for one day? For he had watched his father make the idol.

Then in came a woman with a bowl of meal that she laid in front of the idols to please them. Then Abram thought, This is ridiculous. He picked up a crowbar and smashed all the idols except for the biggest.

When Terah came home he saw the idols lying in fragments, and he said to Abram, "What have you done?"

"I have done nothing," said Abram. "But not long ago a woman came in with a bowl of meal for the idols. And the biggest one said, 'I shall eat from it first.' And another said, 'No, I shall eat from it first,' and they all fell to quarreling, so the biggest idol picked up a stick and smashed the others."

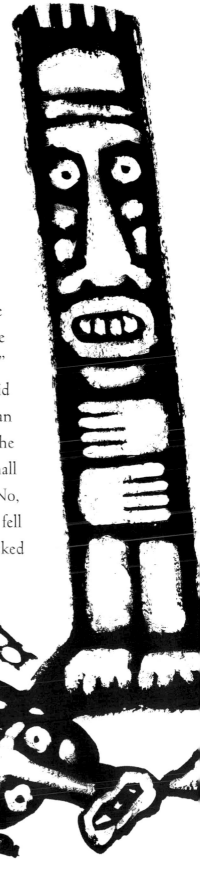

Terah said, "Are you trying to tell me that these things can think?"

And Abram said, "If they cannot think, why do you worship them? What can they do?"

God was watching all this and he said to himself: *Now, this is a man of good sense. Here at last is a man who is all I hoped he would be. I am like a king who loses a precious jewel in the sand. The king orders the sand to be sieved until he finds his jewel again. I have sifted among all men on earth, and I have found my jewel, Abram.*

So he said to Abram: *I have a plan for you. Take your family and leave this place, and I will give you a new land to live in. Your children and your children's children and their children after them shall become a great nation. As you worship me, so shall I take care of you.*

So Abram took his wife, Sarai, and his nephew, Lot, and all those others who believed in God and not in idols, and they went where God had sent them, into a land called Canaan. Abram believed the promise that God had made to him, although he and his wife had not even one child yet.

Now, Abram and Lot between them had so many sheep and cattle that there was not enough grazing for all, and their herdsman and shepherds began to fight.

Then Abram said to his nephew Lot, "Let us not fight but agree to part in peace. We will go our separate ways and you may have first choice." For Abram was a just and generous man, as God had noticed.

So Lot went into the fertile land beyond the river Jordan, and settled there; Abram and Sarai were left in Canaan, to follow their herds and live in tents. And God saw.

49

And God said to Abram: *Look all around you. This shall be yours, and here shall your children become a great nation. Wherever you walk, the land is yours.*

And Abram built an altar to God and worshipped him, and never said, "Lord, what do you mean? How can my children and their children's children become a great nation?"

For he was no longer young, and his wife was not young, and they had no children at all.

The Cities
on the Plain

THE YEARS PASSED AND the years passed and still
no child was born.

And Abram feared that the promise that
he and God had made could not be kept. For
how could his children and his children's
children worship God, when he had no
children? So he chose an heir from his nephew's
family.

But God knew of his fear and spoke to
Abram, saying: *Wait.*

Abram, said God, *I shall keep my promise.*
Your heir will be your own son, and the children

53

of his children shall be as many as the sand on the shore, as the stars in the sky. All that will happen in the future, I know already. Those children shall be strangers in a strange land, and wherever they live they shall be loyal to that land, but they will still be my people and I shall be their God.

米

But Sarai saw the years pass and the years pass and knew only that her husband longed for the son that she could not give him.

So she said to Abram, "Here is Hagar, my maid, who is young. Make her your second wife and she will surely bear you a son."

And Abram so longed for a son that he did as she said.

"Poor Sarai," said Hagar, when she knew that she was pregnant. "How sorry I am for you."

And Sarai was sorry too that she had been so generous, for Hagar's baby was a son, and Sarai had no hope for a child of her own. But Abram thought only, At last! This is the beginning of the great nation that God promised me. And he named his son Ishmael.

Then God said to Abram: *Not yet. The son I promised you shall be the child of your wife Sarai. I have new names for you both. You shall be Abraham, father of nations, and she shall be Sarah, the princess. And next year you will both have a son, and call him Isaac.*

Abraham said, "What about Ishmael?"

God said: *Ishmael too shall be the father of a great nation, and his sons shall be princes. But as to our promise, Abraham, wait for Isaac.*

And Abraham waited.

But God had one thing more to do first, for as in the days before the great flood, the world was going from bad to worse, and worst of all were the cities on the plain where Lot was living. And worst of the worst was the city of Sodom.

55

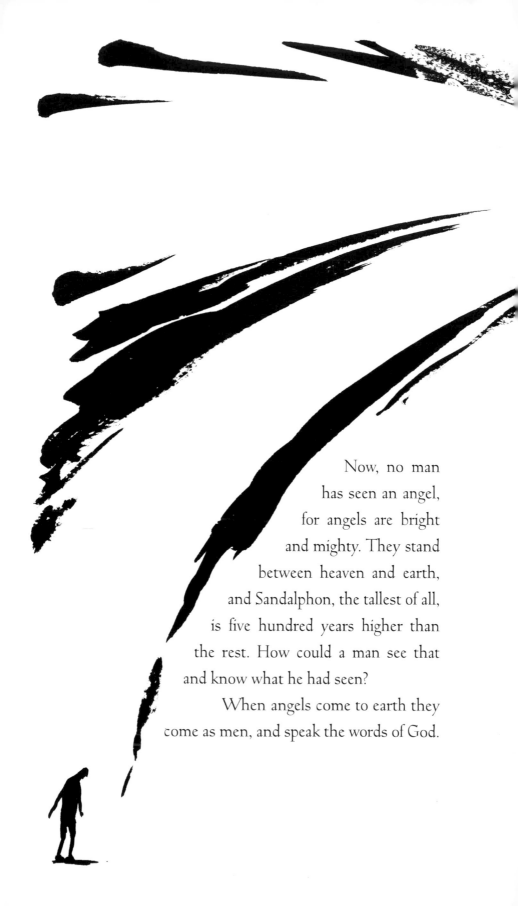

Now, no man
has seen an angel,
for angels are bright
and mighty. They stand
between heaven and earth,
and Sandalphon, the tallest of all,
is five hundred years higher than
the rest. How could a man see that
and know what he had seen?

When angels come to earth they
come as men, and speak the words of God.

As Abraham sat in the doorway of his tent at noon, he saw three workmen approaching: a baker, a seaman, and a traveler. And although they were common men and Abraham was now a great chief, he welcomed them kindly and asked them to stay for a meal in his home.

And Sarah prepared a fine feast for the strangers, and they sat down with Abraham and only seemed to eat (for they were angels, and angels neither eat nor drink upon earth).

Then the angel who was Michael said,

57

"I have come to tell you that your wife will soon bear a son." And Sarah, in the tent, laughed at the very thought, for she was now an old woman.

But the angel said to Sarah, "I have promised you a son and a son you shall have." And Sarah laughed no more.

Then Michael returned to heaven, for his work was done, but the other two men said to Abraham, "Show us the way to the cities on the plain," and Abraham walked with his guests a little distance to show them the way. He did not know that they were Gabriel and Raphael, the angels of God, but Abraham was courteous to workmen and angels alike.

And God looked down at his good servant Abraham and said to himself: *I am about to do a terrible thing, but Abraham deserves to know of it. What will he say when I tell him?*

And God said to Abraham: *The cities on the plain are filled with cruelty and evil. I am going to destroy those cities.*

And Abraham said, "Lord, there may be some good people there among the wicked ones.

Will you destroy them too? Did you not promise long ago that never again would the earth be destroyed?"

And God said: *I promised never to flood it again. Fire, this time.*

Abraham said, "If there are fifty good people in those cities will you spare everyone for their sake?"

And God said: *For fifty will I spare them.*

Abraham said, "Oh, Lord, I am unworthy to ask, but if you will spare them for fifty, why not for forty-five?"

And God said: *Very well. Forty-five.*

Abraham said, "Oh, Lord, do not be angry, but suppose there were thirty? . . ."

And God said: *For thirty good men will I spare the cities.*

Abraham said, "Oh, Lord, for twenty— for *ten?*"

And God said: *Abraham, if I find only ten good men I will spare those cities.*

Would God find ten good men in all of five cities? In Sodom guests were robbed by their

59

hosts and fined by the courts if they complained, for even the judges were called Forger, Liar, Habitual Liar, and Master of Deceit. Kindness carried the death penalty. Generous people were burned alive. And strangers were hated, as Gabriel and Raphael found out.

For when they came to the city of Sodom they were met by Abraham's nephew, Lot. Lot had lived many years with Abraham and had not forgotten how to treat strangers, so when he saw the two men, as he thought, alone in the city at dusk, he said, "Come to my house at once, and stay all night. It is not safe to linger in the street."

So they went in with him and as soon as the door was shut, the men of Sodom, old and young, rioted around the house, shouting, "Who have you got in there? Bring them out!"

So Lot went out and said, "These are my guests. Leave them in peace."

And the men of the city grew violent and cried, "You are a foreigner yourself. Bring out these men or we break down the door."

Then Gabriel and Raphael opened the door and pulled Lot inside. And they said to him, urgently, "Gather your family together and leave the city as soon as day breaks, for God has sent us to destroy it."

Then Raphael led Lot and his family to safety, but Gabriel stayed behind to destroy the city as God had ordered.

And the cities were burned, and everything around them; burned and destroyed. And every living thing perished upon the plain.

And Abraham, standing at the altar where he worshipped God, smelled the fire and saw the rising smoke, and knew that in all the land there had been not even ten good men.

But God kept his promise to Abraham and Sarah, and after a year their son Isaac was born. And Sarah, who had laughed in disbelief, laughed for joy and said, "All the world will laugh with me."

But God remembered Ishmael, the first son of Abraham, and Hagar his mother; and he let Sarah drive them away, for now her son Isaac was the heir of Abraham.

And when Abraham wept and would refuse, God said: *Let them go. Isaac is your heir to be sure, but I promised great things for Ishmael, too. Trust me.*

And Abraham, trusting God, as always, sent Hagar and Ishmael away, into the desert, with only a loaf of bread and a bottle of water. And God sent an angel to keep them from harm.

Ishmael became an archer, and his mother found him a wife, and his sons were great princes, as God had promised.

Now, when Ishmael and Hagar went away, Isaac was four years old.

And Abraham held a feast to celebrate, for his son was weaned and strong, and at last

63

he saw how he and Sarah might be the father and mother of a great nation.

But up in heaven the angels watched with God; and Samael, the fallen angel, turned to God and said, "Look at that! You gave a son to that old man, and there he is, feasting with his friends, and he has not made a single offering to you. He has not even sacrificed a dove. Is that gratitude?"

But God knew that Abraham was grateful in his heart and said: *He is doing it all for the sake of his son. And listen, Samael, if I asked him for an offering, he would give me anything. If I asked him to sacrifice his own son to me, he would do it.*

He was in no hurry, but in his own good time, when Isaac was a young man, God went down to test Abraham one last time.

God said: *Abraham.*

Abraham said, "Lord, here I am."

And God said: *Abraham, take your son, your son Isaac, whom you love dearly, and travel with him into the mountains. And kill him.*

Sons and Brothers

GOD WENT INTO THE mountains of Moriah and waited for Abraham. It was three days' journey for a man, and who knows what Abraham was thinking? But God never doubted that he would come.

The next morning Abraham rose early and saddled his donkey, and with Isaac his son, and two servants, he rode to the mountains, three days' journey.

And on the third day Abraham looked up and saw the place where God was waiting.

"Stay here with the donkey," he said to

his servants, for they had seen nothing. "I go with my son to make a sacrifice to God."

Then Isaac took wood for the fire and followed his father up the mountain. Abraham carried flints in his hand to light the fire; and a knife.

And Isaac said, "Father, we have the wood and the flints, but where is the lamb for the sacrifice?"

And Abraham said, "Oh, my son, God will send us a lamb." But he trusted God and that was all he said.

And when they were upon the mountainside, Abraham lifted rocks and built an altar, and laid the firewood upon the altar. And he looked at his son Isaac; and Isaac knew what the sacrifice must be.

And Isaac said, "Father, when I lie on the altar, bind my hands and feet. For when I see the knife I may struggle with fear and spoil the sacrifice."

And Abraham bound his son Isaac and laid him upon the altar and raised his knife.

Now, God was watching, and all around him the angels wept and cried, "How can this be?" And Samael, who knew full well, went down and stood behind Abraham, jeering, "This is your beloved son, the son of your old age, the son that God promised you. Are you really going to kill him?"

But God saw that whatever Samael said, Abraham would trust in his Lord, so he called to him: *Stop.*

Abraham, said God, *now I know that our promise is safe in your keeping, and in Isaac's after you.*

And when Abraham looked around he saw that God had sent a fine ram for the sacrifice. He would have seen it sooner but Samael was hiding it.

And as the ram was sacrificed, God said to Abraham: *Now you will truly be the father of a great nation.*

And Abraham went back to his servants and they began the journey home.

But Isaac went down another way. Who knows what he thought?

And Samael, in a rage, went swift to the tent of Sarah, the mother of Isaac, and called out, "Hear my news! Your husband has taken your son and killed him for a sacrifice upon the altar."

And Sarah cried out three times and fell dead of grief. That was all Samael's revenge. He got no good of it.

So the son of Abraham lived, and his wife died, and when Abraham came home he wept for her and bought a plot of land where he might bury her. And so Sarah rested in peace.

Why did God ask men for burnt offerings? He did not, but he said: *If they want to sacrifice, better they sacrifice to me than to idols. At least I notice.*

And now it was time to begin the great nation.

So Abraham called to his servant and said, "I am a stranger in this land, but my son must marry a woman of my own people. Go you back to my country and find a wife for my son Isaac."

71

And the servant said, "How if she will not come? Must I take your son to her instead."

Then Abraham said, "No. This is the land God gave to me for myself and my son and the sons of my son. Here he must stay. But God will send an angel before you and the angel will lead you to the bride of my son."

For God had already chosen a wife for Isaac. Back in the land where Abraham was born, there lived the family of Abraham's brother Nahor. And Nahor had a daughter named Rebekah.

When Abraham's servant arrived with his camels, he prayed, "Oh, Lord God, let the girl who comes out to draw water from the well be the one whom I am seeking."

And the angel stood by Rebekah, although she did not know it, and led her out to the well where Abraham's servant waited. And when the servant told of his errand, to find a wife for the son of his master, Rebekah's family let her go gladly to marry the son of their kinsman Abraham.

So Abraham lived to see his sons married, and then he died. Ishmael came back from his new home and with his brother, Isaac, they buried their father beside Sarah his wife.

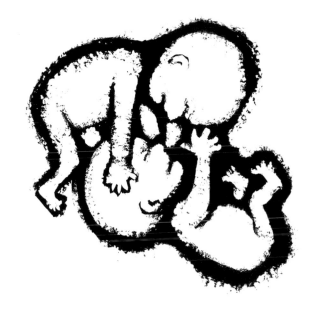

God sent Isaac and Rebekah twin sons. They fought before they were born, they were born fighting, and ever after they could never agree. Esau was a hunter, but Jacob was a quiet man and lived at home. Esau was his father's favorite, but Rebekah loved Jacob the most.

73

Now, Esau was the elder but God knew that from Jacob would come the great nation that he had promised to Abraham.

And one day Esau came home weary and famished from hunting and he saw his brother, Jacob, cooking lentils, by his tent.

Esau said, "Give me some of that, or I die of hunger."

74

Jacob said, "Only if you give me your birthright in exchange."

And Esau agreed to sell his inheritance for a bowl of soup.

Perhaps they were joking, who knows? But God heard their promise and held them to it.

And when Isaac grew old he wanted to bless his first-born, Esau. But Jacob and his mother tricked Isaac, who was blind, and he gave the blessing to Jacob, and God allowed it.

Then Esau swore to kill Jacob his brother, and Rebekah said to Jacob, "Your life is in danger. Leave here and seek refuge with my brother Laban, until it is safe to come home."

She thought he would be gone for a few days, but he did not come home again for twenty years.

Now, on the first night that Jacob fled from Esau, he slept on bare earth with stones for his pillow. And God sent him a dream of a ladder that stood between earth and heaven, with angels going up and down on it.

God stood at the top of the ladder and called to Jacob: *I am the God of your father, Isaac, and of his father, Abraham. And I will be your God also. I will give to you the land where you lie now. It shall be yours, and your sons', and all who come after them; but wherever else you may go, I will go with you, and I will not leave you until all that I promise you is done.*

And when Jacob awoke he knew that God had been there with him, and he made a vow, saying, "If God does all that he has promised, and cares for me, and keeps me safe, then truly, he shall be my God."

Then Jacob went on eastward, until he came to the land where his uncle Laban lived. And when he saw Laban's daughter Rachel he loved her at once and asked to marry her.

Laban said, "Yes, if you work for me for seven years."

And Jacob loved Rachel so much that the seven years seemed as short as seven days.

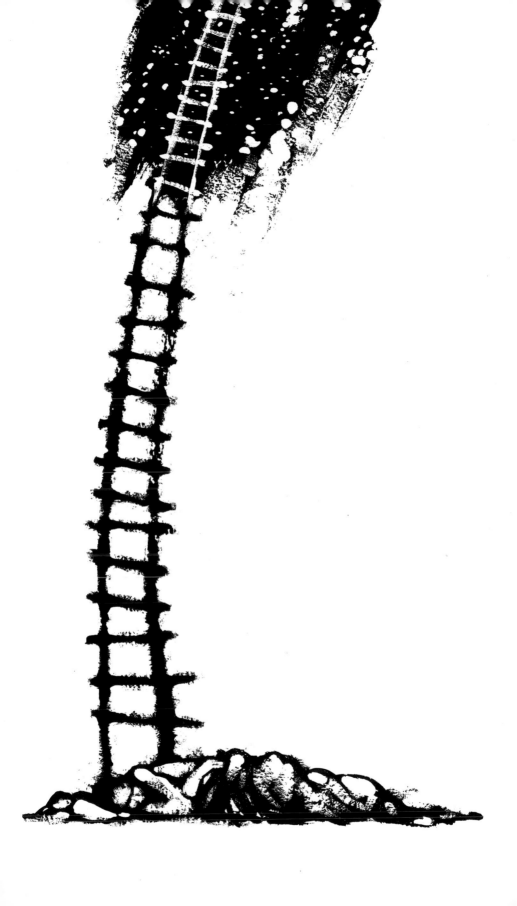

But at the end of the seven years, Laban tricked Jacob, as Jacob had tricked Isaac, and married him to his elder daughter, Leah. For he thought, It is her turn first to marry.

Jacob swore to serve another seven years for Rachel, and Laban agreed.

Did Jacob think that God had forgotten his promise? God knew that one day he would have need of Rachel's children, but from Leah's children would come the great nation that he had promised to Abraham.

So Leah had four sons and Rachel had none, and Rachel wept.

"Jacob," cried Rachel, "give me children or I shall die."

And Jacob was angry. "Am I God?" he said. "If you cannot have children, what can I do about it?"

Then God was angry too. He said to Jacob: *Is that the way to comfort a woman in distress? One day your children will beg for mercy from her son. Suppose he answers them as you have answered her — 'Am I God?'*

Then God sent Jacob six more sons and a daughter, but Rachel was not their mother. Only when Jacob had four wives and ten sons did God allow Rachel a child at last.

The sons of Jacob were Reuben, Simeon, Levi, and Judah; Dan, Naphtali, and Gad; Asher and Issachar and Zebulun; and his daughter was named Dinah.

The eleventh son was the one that God was waiting for. And Rachel his mother named him Joseph.

The Dreamer in Egypt

Now, JACOB WAS A man who lived by his wits. Laban tricked Jacob into marrying both his daughters. Jacob tricked Laban by taking the best of his sheep.

And God, watching, thought, How hard this man works on his own behalf. He has cheated his brother, he has cheated his father-in-law. But it suits my plan and he has not cheated me.

So God let him get on with it.

Jacob left Laban as he had come to him, on the run. For God told him to return with his family to the land of his father, Isaac, and when Laban pursued him, God kept them apart and made them swear peace before each went his own way.

Then Jacob came to the borders of the land where his brother, Esau, lived, and he sent messengers to make peace with Esau, for twenty years before he had tricked his own brother.

The messengers returned saying, "Esau is coming to meet you with four hundred men."

Then Jacob was afraid, and he said to God, "Now I fear that Esau is coming to kill me and my family. Remember how you promised that my descendants should number thousands? How can that happen if Esau kills my children?"

And in case God did nothing to help him, Jacob divided his sheep and his cattle and his camels, so that even if Esau attacked, he could not take everything.

And he sent his family ahead to safety,
and stayed behind to wait for Esau.

And God sent an angel to wrestle with
Jacob, like a king who taught his son to fight
with a lion, so that he might be a match for any

dog that attacked him. For if an angel could not conquer Jacob, who then could hope to?

All night they struggled and neither could win, although one was a man and the other was an angel. The angel struck Jacob on the thigh, and lamed him, but still Jacob hung on. He was a hard man to outwit, was Jacob.

Then the angel said, "Day breaks and I have business in heaven. Let me go."

And Jacob said, "I will not, unless you bless me."

The angel said, "What is your name?"

And Jacob said, "It is Jacob."

The angel said, "Not any longer. You will be called Israel, for this night you have struggled with God."

Then Jacob knew that he had seen God and that God had not struck him down.

But he walked lame ever afterward.

The next day Esau and Jacob met and made peace, and so Jacob came home at last.

And God came once more to Jacob, to remind him: *Your name is Israel now. And the land*

that I gave to Abraham and Isaac shall be yours.
Your children will be great chiefs of their people.

And after that, Jacob's wife Rachel died, giving birth to her second son. And Jacob-Israel named him Benjamin. This was the last of his twelve sons.

Then Isaac died, and his two sons, Esau and Jacob-Israel, buried him. Esau took his family and his flocks and journeyed away, for now he and his brother had such great possessions there was not room in the land for both of them.

So Jacob-Israel was chief of all his family, in the land of Canaan. He had great wealth and many flocks and his people lived in comfort and plenty, and there seemed no end to these good times.

But God knew that in twenty years famine would ravage the land of Canaan and all the lands around it, even as far as Egypt. And he

85

knew that now was the time to put into action his plan to save the children of Jacob-Israel. That was what Joseph was for, although Joseph did not know it.

Joseph knew only that he was the favorite son of Jacob-Israel, and his elder brothers hated him for it. They hated him for the tales he told against them and for the fine clothes that their father gave him.

By the time that Joseph was seventeen, his brothers wanted only to kill him.

For God sent Joseph dreams, and he dreamed that he would be a great man, by and by. He dreamed that his father and brothers would bow down before him.

He did not know why, but he made sure to tell his brothers.

Now, soon after, the sons of Jacob-Israel were away from home, tending their father's flocks, and God put it into Jacob-Israel's mind to send Joseph to bring back word about them.

So Joseph went off, without asking directions, and wandered astray in the fields.

God said: *Look, now he is getting lost. Go down, Gabriel, and set him on the right road.*

So Joseph met a man in a field who told him where to find his brothers, and Joseph never knew that he had talked with an angel.

And when the brothers saw Joseph in the distance, they said to one another, "Look, here comes the dreamer."

And then they said, "Let us kill him and see what becomes of his dreams."

But Reuben, the eldest, said, "No. Let us throw him into a deep pit and say that he is dead." For he thought, I cannot kill my own brother. Later I will come back to the pit and rescue him.

But when Joseph was in the pit, Judah had a better idea.

"Here come traders of Ishmael's tribe," said Judah. "Let us sell Joseph to them, for a slave."

So the Ishmaelites paid cash for Joseph and took him with them to Egypt, which was where God intended that he should go. That was his plan for Joseph. Almost it had not worked.

Then the brothers took Joseph's fine coat and dipped it in goat's blood, and went with it to Jacob-Israel.

"This seems to be Joseph's coat," they said. "He seems to be dead. How sad."

And Jacob-Israel knew the coat that he had given to his favorite son, and he wept, and no one could comfort him.

Meanwhile, in Egypt, Joseph was a slave in a great man's house. And he did very well until he offended the great man's wife, and the great man put him in jail.

There he met servants of Pharaoh who had angered their king. Each dreamed a dream and Joseph told them that one man's dream foretold his death. And so it did. And he was hanged. But the other man's dream foretold his release.

And when this servant was set free, Joseph said to him, "I am an innocent man. Remember to plead for me when you leave this prison."

But the man forgot Joseph for two whole years. God thought that it would do Joseph no harm to learn that he should trust his God instead of other men.

Then, Pharaoh of Egypt dreamed a dream and none could tell what it meant. And only then did the servant remember Joseph.

So Joseph was brought up from prison and Pharaoh told him of his dream.

And Joseph said, "It is a dream of famine. God has shown Pharaoh what is to come. For seven years Egypt will have good crops, but after that come seven years of hunger. You must find a wise man to fill the granaries during the good years, so that the people may have food while the famine lasts."

The Pharaoh cried, "If your God has made you so wise then you must be that man."

And Pharaoh made Joseph a governor over the people, and Joseph became a great man, and Joseph thought that he had done well for himself. But what had Joseph done? God had done it all, and not for Joseph's sake, and not for the sake of Egypt, but for the sake of his promise to Abraham.

For when the famine came to Canaan, Jacob-Israel heard that there was corn in Egypt and sent his sons to buy supplies. But he kept Benjamin with him, his last son and his dearest, now that Joseph was gone.

91

The Plagues
and the Passover

So long as Joseph lived, and his friend Pharaoh lived, the children of Israel were safe in the land of Egypt. They forgot why they were there and who had sent them. Life was easy.

But Pharaoh died, and his son after him, and the son of his son; and at last a pharaoh sat upon the throne of Egypt who did not remember Joseph. This king looked about him and saw the children of Israel among the Egyptians, and he said, "There are too many of these people. Soon there will be more of them than there are of us. If we go to war they may side with our enemies."

So the Egyptians turned on the children of Israel and made them into slaves.

Then Pharaoh said, "There are still too many, they have too many children. Let them keep their daughters, but when a son is born take the baby and kill it."

So the children of Israel suffered and wept and, although they did not call to God, God heard them and remembered the promise that he had made to Abraham. And he looked for a way to keep his promise and save his people.

There was a woman of Levi's family who had two children already, Miriam and Aaron. And when her second son was born she hid him in a box among the reeds in the river. The daughter of Pharaoh herself found the box and took out the baby and kept him as her own son. She told people, "I drew him out of the water." Now, the word for that is *moses* and that was how he was known.

Moses grew up as an Egyptian prince, but he killed a man who was beating an Israelite slave, and fled for his life to the distant land of Midian. And there he married a girl called Zipporah and worked for her father, Jethro, herding sheep and goats, as Jacob had worked for Laban, long ago. But Jethro was an honest man, and so was Moses. And God watched him.

97

One day a kid ran away from the flock and Moses went after it. At last it came to a pool of water and stopped to drink, and Moses, quite worn out, caught up with it. But he was not angry. He said, "I did not know that you needed a drink so badly, and now you must be tired as well." So he lifted the little goat onto his shoulder and carried it home.

And God said: *That is a good shepherd. I shall make him the shepherd of my flock, Israel.*

Now, Moses had been a prince and chose to live as a humble man, and God saw that he would never think of himself as a leader. And God wondered, How can I talk to this man? If I speak quietly he will not know that it is God who calls him, but if I shout I may frighten him.

Then God said to the angel Michael: *Go down to the mountainside and burn like a fire in that thornbush. But do not let the bush be burned away.*

So Michael went down in blazing flames, and when Moses, walking by with his flock, saw the bush that burned but did not turn to ash, he went to look at this strange sight.

And as he came close, God spoke to him, not quietly, not loudly, but in the voice of a man, like a father speaking to his son. God said: *Moses, Moses.*

And Moses said, "Here I am."

God said: *I am your God, the God of Abraham and Isaac and Jacob.* And Moses believed that it was indeed God who spoke, and hid his face in fear.

Then God said: *You have seen how the people of Israel suffer in Egypt and so have I. Now I am going to save them from Pharaoh and bring them back to the land I gave to Abraham. And I have chosen you to go to Pharaoh and tell him this.*

Moses said, "Why should he listen to me?"

God said: *I will go with you.*

And Moses said, "But who shall I say sent me? What do I call you? What is your name?"

And God said: *I have different names for all the things that I do and all the things that I am. I am called God, and I am called Almighty God when I judge people, and I am called the Lord of Armies when I fight with wickedness, and I am called Adonai when I am merciful. Therefore my name is I AM, for I am what I do, but never speak that name aloud. Call me Adonai, the merciful, instead. Now, go to the Israelites and tell them that their God, the God of Abraham, will take them home to the land that was promised to them.*

And then God said: *After that, go to Pharaoh, and tell him the same thing. But, Moses, I have to warn you; I do not think that Pharaoh will let my people go. And if he refuses I shall not be merciful to Pharaoh.*

Moses said, "Lord, I do not think that anyone is going to believe any of this."

Then God gave Moses a staff of wood and turned it into a serpent, and back again. *They will believe a miracle,* God said. *Take the staff with you.*

But Moses said, "O Lord, I do not speak well. No one will listen to me. Send someone who will do it properly."

Then God lost patience with Moses and said: *I have chosen you, and I happen to know that your brother, Aaron, speaks very well indeed. I will tell you what to say and you can tell Aaron what to say, and Aaron can say it. Now go — and take that staff with you.*

So Moses said farewell to his family and returned to Egypt.

And at the very same time he spoke to Moses on the mountain in Midian, God spoke to Aaron in Egypt and said: *Your brother is coming home. Go to meet him.*

And when Aaron and Moses met, Moses told his brother of his talk with God, and together they went to the leaders of the people of Israel. And Moses told Aaron what to say, and Aaron said it.

And then the people of Israel stopped work, for they knew that their God had not forgotten them, and they bowed their heads in worship.

And after that, Moses and Aaron went to Pharaoh and said, "The Lord God of Israel has sent us to tell you to set his people free and let them go."

Pharaoh said, "I have never heard of this God of Israel. Who is he?" And he said to his servants, "Go to the library and look him up." And then he said, "Our slaves are standing idle. Make them work even harder; give them impossible tasks."

Then the leaders of Israel went to Moses and Aaron and said, "Now look at what you have done."

And Moses said to God, "Things are

worse than they were before. Pharaoh has not let the people go and you have not saved them and everyone says that it is my fault."

But God said to Moses: *My children are obstinate and bad tempered. If you become their leader, do not expect them to thank you. Now go with Aaron to Pharaoh and take that staff I gave you. And if Pharaoh refuses to let the people go, tell Aaron to hold out the staff over the river. And the water in the river, and all the water in Egypt, will turn to blood. For now it is Pharaoh's turn to suffer as my people have suffered.*

So Moses and Aaron went to Pharaoh as God had commanded, and Aaron held out his staff over the river, and all the water in Egypt was turned into blood.

And still Pharaoh did not let the people go. So God said to Moses: *Tell Aaron to hold out the staff over the streams, and I will send a plague of frogs to cover the land of Egypt.*

Moses and Aaron did as they were told, and God sent clammy frogs from one end of the land to the other, and the biggest frog sat on the throne in Pharaoh's palace, but Pharaoh would not let the people go.

Then God said to Moses: *Tell Aaron to beat the staff upon the ground and the dust shall become a plague of lice.* And after the plague of lice, God sent a swarm of flies, and after the swarm of flies, he sent a sickness that killed the cattle, but still Pharaoh would not let the people go.

Then God said: *It is too late now for Pharaoh to change his mind.* And God sent boils to plague the people of Egypt, and he threw down hail like thunderstones to ruin the crops, and then he sent locusts to eat what was left. And after the locusts came three days of darkness, thick as tar, so that no one could move in it.

Then God said to Moses: *I shall bring one more plague upon Egypt, for as Pharaoh killed your sons, so shall I kill the first-born of the Egyptians. Tell the people of Israel to stay in their houses and roast a lamb for supper. Tell them to mark their doors with the blood of the lamb. And tell them to make their bread dough without yeast tonight, as there will be no time for it to rise. For tonight I shall save my people. The angel of death will pass through this land and the first-born of Egypt will die. But where you have made the sign upon your doorposts, the angel of death will pass over you, and every year from now on, you will remember this night and keep the Passover Feast.*

Then Moses called the leaders of the people together and told them what God had said. And after the nine plagues they knew that Moses and Aaron spoke the truth, and they in their turn told the people how the tenth plague would pass over them.

So the people went home to roast their lambs and make their unleavened bread and mark their doors. And they waited, dressed for traveling, all night long, while the angel of death passed through the land of Egypt.

And they heard cries of grief in every house, for in every house someone had died, and in the king's house the son of Pharaoh too lay dead.

And in the night Pharaoh sent for Moses and Aaron and said, "Go."

And the people of Egypt said to the people of Israel, "Go; go from among us before we are all dead men."

And so the people of Israel left Egypt, six hundred thousand on foot, and all their herds and flocks and cattle.

And God said: *Now Pharaoh of Egypt knows who I am.*

The Gift of Torah

THE WAY TO CANAAN lay through the land of the
Philistines, who were at war. So God thought, I
will lead the people by another way in case they
try to return to Egypt, saying, "Better the trouble
we knew than the trouble we do not know."

And to guide the people God sent an
angel ahead of them that seemed like a tall cloud
by day and a column of fire by night.

But when the people of Israel came to the
Red Sea, they looked back and saw that
Pharaoh had changed his mind again, for
coming after them was the army of Egypt—

soldiers, horsemen, and chariots—led by Pharaoh himself.

And the people of Israel turned upon Moses and cried, "Did you bring us out of Egypt to die here in the wilderness? Better the trouble we knew than the trouble we do not know."

But God said to Moses: *Tell the people to go forward. And when you come to the sea, hold out your staff, and the waters will draw back for you.*

Then God sent a great wind from the east and the waters of the Red Sea parted, and the people went across dry-shod. And after them came Pharaoh with his warriors and his chariots, and God waited until they were half-way across before he said to Moses: *Hold out your staff again.*

And as Moses did it, God let the waters return in a towering wave, and that was the end of Pharaoh and all his army.

Then the angels in heaven began to praise God for saving his people, but God said: *This is no time for singing. Egyptians or not, those are men down there, men that I made, and they are dying.*

Still, he allowed Moses and the people to praise him, and Miriam, the sister of Moses and Aaron, led the women in a dance of joy.

But after three days, when the angel had led them into the wilderness, they could find no water and the unleavened bread ran out; and the people turned on Moses and said, "We were better off in Egypt."

And Moses, in despair, said, "Lord, do you hear them?"

And God said: *Yes, I do. I hear them as well as I hear you, so there is no need to pray to me on their behalf. Tell Aaron to tell them that I shall send them food from heaven every morning, and they can gather it up. And you, Moses, shall bring water out of a dry rock by striking it with the staff. They will like that.*

So every morning after that, except on the seventh day, God sent food from heaven and the people gathered it up and called it *manna*. But on the seventh day they rested, as God himself had rested after he made the world and all that was in it.

Now, the journey from Egypt to Canaan is eleven
days on foot, but after two months the angel of
God still led the people around and about in the
wilderness. For God thought, If I were a king with
a small son I would not give him my wealth while
he was a child and could not take care of it. I
would wait until he was grown up and educated
and then he should have it all. If I bring Israel into
their promised land at once, they will not know

113

what to do. I will give them laws to live by, and teach them how to keep those laws, and only then will I give them their land.

And as the people of Israel followed the angel in the wilderness, enemies attacked them. And Moses chose a young man, Joshua, to be his war chief and lead the people against the enemy. And all through the battle, Moses stood upon a hill and held out his staff so that Joshua and his warriors would know that God was with them. And the people of Israel won.

Then Jethro, the father-in-law of Moses, came to join the people of Israel.

And he saw how the people came to Moses, day in, day out, to ask for advice, and Jethro said, "This is all too much for you. You must appoint others to help you, to judge the people, and show them how to live."

Then God saw that the people of Israel were ready to be given laws to live by, and he said to Moses: *I am going to give you my Torah.*

This is the Law of Living, and it existed before the first day of time. Tell the people that in three days

you and I will meet upon Mount Sinai, and I shall
give you Torah.

And on the third day the mountain was
covered in smoke and God came down in fire
and flame, and the people heard the voice of

God telling them the laws by which they must live. Never again would people have to ask what they must do or how they ought to do it. God had thought of everything, what they should do and what they should not.

And when God had spoken he said: *Moses, write it all down and make sure that the people understand what I have said. I have given them six hundred and thirteen commandments, but they cannot take those in all at once, so I will give you two slabs of stone, and on these you and I will write ten commandments for the people to obey. Come alone to the mountaintop and meet me.*

And on the mountaintop God said to Moses: *Once Torah was in heaven. I have given it to you, but I cannot part with it, so now I must come down to earth with my law. Make me a tent in which to live when I come among you. Make a beautiful box where we can keep Torah, and put on it a mercy seat where I, Adonai, will sit. And make me a great candlestick of seven branches. Make an altar where I may receive burnt offerings, and when the people worship me, Aaron shall be High Priest.*

Now I will tell you how to make all those things.

And the telling of that took forty days, and when God had finished, Moses said, "Lord, who is going to do all this?"

God said: *There is a man of Judah's tribe called Bezalel. Give him my instructions — he will make the tent and the box, the mercy seat, the altar, the candlestick, and the robes of the High Priest.*

Then God gave Moses two stone slabs with ten laws on them to take back to the people.

Now, while Moses was away on the mountain the people grew restless and thought that their leader had left them and that God had forgotten them.

So to keep them quiet, Aaron collected their earrings and melted these down to make an idol for the people to worship. And Samael saw, and said to God, "Look what happens as soon as you take your eyes off them."

Moses and God looked down and saw the
people of Israel worshipping their idol. And God
said to Moses: *The first commandment I gave your
people was this: You shall have no other gods but me.
And the first thing they have done is make an idol.*

Moses said, "Lord, when the people do
right, they are *your* people, but when they do
wrong they are *my* people. Right or wrong,
Lord, they are yours."

But God said: *You had better get out of
here. I am going to destroy them. It is of no use
trying to stop me.*

And Moses thought, I have not tried to stop him yet. That must mean that he wants me to plead with him. And then he saw the angels of heaven ready to fall upon Israel and destroy the people, and he said, "O Lord, is this all their fault? You could have let them go anywhere in the world, but you sent them to Egypt, where everyone worships idols. They were bound to pick up bad habits; what did you expect? Anyway, you have always known what they were like. Why punish them now?"

So God held back the angels and Moses went down the mountain with the slabs of stone, but when he came among the people and saw the idol up close, he was so enraged that he flung down the slabs of stone, and they broke.

And God said: *Now who is angry?*

Moses said, "You were angry first."

God said: *There is no point in both of us being angry. We had better take turns so that I can calm you and you can calm me.* And he gave to Moses two new slabs of stone with the ten commandments written upon them.

119

Then all the people brought gold and jewels and fine cloth and furs and leather. And Bezalel made them into a box for the stones of the Law, and the candlestick, and the mercy seat, and the altar, and the tent where God might live when he came among his people.

And Moses said, "Lord, all earth and seven heavens are not large enough to hold you. How will you get into that tent?"

God said: *If I want to, I can fit into a space one cubit square.*

And when the people of Israel followed the tall cloud by day and the column of fire by night, they folded away the tent and the altar and carried them along with the candlestick and the box where the Law was kept. And when they camped they set up the tent and the altar, and God came into the tent unseen, and rested upon the mercy seat. And Moses and Aaron taught the laws to the people.

And the people complained that being chosen by God was harder than being forgotten. And God said: *Quite so. I have given*

you my Torah and asked for nothing in return—except that you keep the commandments. They are my receipt.

But the people thought that six hundred and thirteen commandments were too many to remember. And God said: *Quite so. That is why I told Moses to get them down to ten so that you would have no trouble learning them immediately. And I shall be much harder on you, my chosen people, than on anyone else, if you fail me.*

The Battle for Canaan

Now, as the people of Israel wandered in the wilderness, God led them near to the borders of Canaan, for he thought, They are not ready to enter their promised land, but they may as well see what I am going to give them.

So God said to Moses: *Choose one man from each tribe of Israel and send them to look at the land of Canaan.*

Now, the tribes were named after the sons of Jacob-Israel: Reuben, Simeon, and Judah; Dan, Naphtali, and Gad; Asher, Issachar, Zebulun, Benjamin; and Ephraim and Manassah, the sons of Joseph. There was no tribe of Levi's name, for the Levites were priests, with Aaron.

And Moses chose twelve men to go as spies into Canaan, and also he sent Joshua, his war chief, for God meant Joshua to be the leader of Israel, after Moses.

Now, the spies went into Canaan and saw that it was rich and fertile, but they also saw that the people of Canaan were fierce and strong, and they were afraid that they would be made to fight for the land. So when they came back to Moses and Aaron, they said, "This land is a terrible place, filled with giants. Let us leave it alone."

124

And all the people were afraid and said, "Moses and Aaron have led us into danger. Let us stone them to death and choose new leaders and go back to Egypt, where we were safe."

And God thought, What short memories they have.

But Joshua and Caleb, the spy from Judah's tribe, said, "No! This is a wonderful land and if God is with us we can conquer it now. We will lead you."

But the people said, "Let us kill all four of them and return to Egypt."

Then God came down into his tent that Bezalel had made, and said to Moses: *How much longer do I have to put up with this? I have had enough of their ingratitude. I shall take back my Law and they shall have no land. Instead I shall send a plague to wipe them out.*

But Moses cried, "O Lord, no. Think what people will say. They will believe that you did not lead us into Canaan because you could not. The people deserve to be punished, but be merciful instead. Be Adonai to us."

125

And because it was Moses who pleaded with him, God said: *Very well. But now I shall make you stay out in this wilderness for forty years, and no one who was grown up when he left Egypt shall live to enter the Promised Land, except for Joshua and Caleb who had faith in me.*

Moses said, "Lord, does that mean me and Aaron too?"

And God said: *At the end of time there will be a new world, and all who have lived and obeyed me will be with me in it. I made you a leader of these people. If I let you enter the Promised Land and leave them behind where they have died in the wilderness, people will think I have abandoned them. Better you stay with them now, and lead them again into the world to come.*

Then Moses told the people what God had said, and the people were sorry for what they had done, but all the same, they were in the wilderness for forty years, and for forty years they had to fight for their lives with the tribes who lived around them. And Joshua led them to victory.

Miriam died, and Aaron died, and at last there was only Moses left, who had led the people out of Egypt. And the day came when Moses said to the people of Israel, "I am an old man and for forty years I have led you in the wilderness. Now it is time for you to enter Canaan, the land God promised to you, but I cannot go with you. So remember all that you have learned with me, remember the laws that God has given you, and remember the promise that God made to our ancestor, Abraham. But remember this above all. God is merciful, God is just, God is angry, and God is compassionate. God is many things and all things, but there is only one of him. Hear, O Israel; Adonai, our God, is one God."

And then Moses placed his hand upon the shoulder of Joshua and said, "Joshua is your leader now and from today you will follow him, over the river of Jordan, into the Promised Land."

But Moses went with God, up into the mountains overlooking the land of Canaan, and God said: *There it is, the land I promised to*

Abraham and to the people of Israel, but you may only look, you may not go over the Jordan with your people.

And Moses said, "Lord, I never wanted to be a leader in the first place, and I never asked to enter Canaan anyway. The whole thing was your idea from the start. Is my death some kind of punishment? And if so, what have I done?"

God said: *Moses, you are dying because all men must die, since the first man, Adam, disobeyed me. Even Abraham died at last, even Isaac and Jacob, who wrestled with my angel. But Moses, when other men die, their kinsmen and friends attend their funerals. I, myself, and all my angels, will attend to yours.*

Then Moses died upon the mountain, and Samael lurked nearby, waiting to steal away his soul, but God himself, with Gabriel and Michael, put Moses in the tomb and laid him to rest.

So no man knows where Moses lies, but they say of him still: In all the world, there was never a man like Moses, for the Lord God spoke to Moses as a man talks to his friend.

129

Then Joshua crossed the Jordan River and the people followed him, for God said to Joshua: *Be strong, be courageous. This land is yours for the taking. Go, take it, and I will be with you.*

And Joshua said to the people, "This is the land that God has given to us, even as Moses told you."

And then, for many years, Joshua and the armies of Israel fought the kings and the tribes of Canaan, and there were tales of great battles and thousands killed. But perhaps the tales were greater than the battles, for when the wars were over there were still many people living in Canaan as well as the people of Israel. And Joshua divided up the land between the twelve tribes.

And Joshua said, "Now I am old and must die and leave you. This is what God has told me. He gave this land to Abraham and now he has given it back to you. He has given you a land for which you did not work, and cities that you did not build. The food that you eat, you did not grow.

"God promised you this land and he has kept his promise. See to it that you keep your promise to him. Live by his Law and do not worship the idols of Canaan."

Then the people promised to serve and obey their God, and Joshua sent them away, every tribe to the land that he had given it.

And so his work was done, and Joshua died.

131

Soon the people forgot their promise and worshipped the idols of Canaan. They forgot that God had brought them out of Egypt and given them the land in which they lived, and they forgot Torah, the Law.

So God called certain leaders to be judges, to bring the people back to the Law, but as soon as each judge was dead, the people went back to forgetting. Forgetting was easier than living by the Law and, anyway, they did not want judges, they wanted a king, like the other peoples of Canaan.

And then God stirred up the enemies of Israel, and when the people of Israel asked him for help, he said: *No, I have had enough. Fight your own battles in the future. If you need help, go and ask the idols of Canaan, since they are the gods you worship now. I dare say they will save you.*

Then the people of Israel knew that the idols of Canaan could do nothing, and they said to God, "We were wrong, and we are sorry. Look, we are turning our backs on the idols."

So then God was sorry for them, as he

always was, and he saved them from their enemies once more. And he sent four strong, honest men to be judges over the people, but when the last of these judges was dead, the people forgot the Law again, and forgot their God, and this time God was not sorry and let the Philistines in to ravage the land for forty years. And the people of Israel fought the Philistines, and they fought one another, and still they wanted a king, like everyone else.

God knew that one day he would send the people of Israel a great king to lead them in battle and to lead them in prayer. But that king was not yet born, and nor was his father, nor his father's father.

But in the town of Bethlehem lived a man of Judah's tribe called Boaz. He was a rich and powerful man, but his cousin Naomi was a poor widow, alone in the world except for Ruth, her daughter-in-law. And Ruth was a widow, too.

Now, Ruth was not one of the people of Israel. She came from Moab, the people of Abraham's nephew, Lot. That was why God saved Lot from Sodom, for God saw to it that Ruth and Boaz should meet and marry. And so they did, and their son was called Obed. And when Obed grew up he married, and his son was called Jesse.

The last judge of Israel was the prophet Samuel, and when he grew old the people said to him, "We want no more judges. Give us a king."

And Samuel told the people what a king would do to them, and how he would take more than he gave. "You will beg God for mercy if he sends you a king," said Samuel, "and he will not listen to you for you have not listened to him."

But the people said, "We want a king like everyone else, to lead us in battle against the Philistines."

Now, God knew that his king would be the son of Jesse, but he was not yet born. Still, he said to Samuel: *You had better give them what they want.*

And God thought, Now I must find someone to rule for a while, until my king is ready.

Saul and David

THE SMALLEST TRIBE of all was the tribe of
Benjamin. No one from that tribe would ever
expect to become king, but God looked down
and saw a young man of Benjamin's people out
searching for this father's donkeys, which had
strayed from home.

Was ever a king found herding donkeys?

But God saw that this man, Saul, was one
that the people would follow, so he leaned down
and whispered in the ear of Samuel the prophet:
About this time tomorrow I shall send you a young
man of Benjamin's tribe. I want you to take oil and

137

pour it on his head as a sign that I have made him leader of Israel, to fight the Philistines in my name.

And the next day Saul came to Samuel's house and God said: *What did I tell you? Here he is, the man I have chosen to be king.*

Then Samuel did as God told him. He anointed Saul with the oil and took him out to show him to the people. And Samuel said, "This is the man that God himself has made king over you."

Then the people looked and saw that God had chosen for their leader a fine handsome man, head and shoulders taller than the tallest among them, and they all cried, "God save the King!" At last they had what they wanted.

But looks are not everything. All was not well in Saul's head. Had God not noticed? Who knows?

Still, Saul made a good start, and there were no idols worshipped while he was king. He raised a great army and fought the Philistines. His son, Jonathan, grew to manhood and fought alongside him until the Philistines were beaten back into their own land, and the people rejoiced, saying, "See what our king has done for us."

But Samuel reminded them, "Saul is your leader on earth, but never forget that God is your leader in heaven." And even though God had sent him many victories, Saul too forgot who had made him what he was. Alone he had not the strength to be king, for his mind was dark and confused.

Then God said to Samuel: *I have a message for Saul. When Moses led the people of Israel out of Egypt, the first enemies that attacked them were the Amalekites. Joshua won that battle, but the Amalekites are still here and they are still strong. Now is the time for Saul to gather his army and wipe them out, once and for all.*

So Samuel went to Saul and said, "God commands you to lead the people against the

139

Amalekites, and slaughter them all so that never again will they trouble the land."

And Saul went out with his army and there was great killing that day. But Saul did not do quite all that God and Samuel told him to, for he spared the life of the Amalekite king, and kept the best of his sheep and cattle.

"What is this mooing and bleating I hear?" Samuel said.

"I meant to sacrifice them to God," said Saul, shiftily. And then he changed his story. "It was the people who took the livestock to sacrifice," said Saul.

Then Samuel said to Saul, "God does not ask for sacrifice. He demands obedience."

Saul said, "I was afraid of what the people would do if I went against their wishes."

Samuel said, "God made you king over the people. He is the one you ought to have feared. But it is too late, you have failed him too often."

Then Saul and Samuel went their separate ways and never met again while they were living.

And God knew that it had been a great mistake to make Saul king over Israel, for his wits were unsteady; but now it was time to prepare the new king, and this time there would be no mistake.

God said to Samuel: *It is no use your grieving over Saul, for I have a new king and you must go and anoint him. You will find him in Bethlehem, among the sons of Jesse, of the tribe of Judah. They are all fine young men, but wait until I tell you who to choose.* For now God knew, and Samuel knew, that looks are not everything.

So Samuel went to Jesse's house and saw his seven sons, one after the other, and each time God said to Samuel, privately: *This is not the one.*

141

At last Samuel said to Jesse, "Are these all your sons?"

And Jesse said, "There is still the youngest but he is out in the hills, watching the sheep."

Was ever a king found herding sheep?

But they sent for the youngest son and when he came in from work God said to Samuel: *This is the one.*

So there in the house, Samuel took oil and anointed the youngest son of Jesse, and so it was that David learned that one day he would be the second king of Israel.

And yet, while Saul lived, David said nothing of this and served his king loyally. He was a brave soldier who killed the strongest of the Philistines; he was a gifted musician and his harp could calm the king when he was wandering in his wits. He was a faithful friend and like a brother to the king's son, Jonathan. The people adored him and praised his victories until Saul, mad and grieving, said, "He has everything except one thing: my crown. He will be after that next."

And Saul hated David and feared him,
and yet David never lifted a hand against his
king. God had promised him the crown. If God
was not ready, David was willing to wait. But he
fled for his life to live among the Philistines.

Then Saul and his son died in battle, and David
mourned for the deaths of his sovereign and his
great friend Jonathan. But now he was king
himself, and he turned to God and said, "What
do you want me to do?"

And whatever God told David to do,
David did it, for he never forgot that it was God

who had made him king. For more than seven years there was war between the followers of David and the followers of Saul, but at last all the tribes of Israel swore loyalty to David, and God saw that once more his people were one people.

Then David took the fortress of Jerusalem and made it the capital of his country. And he fetched home the box that Bezalel had made long ago in the wilderness, at the foot of Mount Sinai, where Moses had placed the two stone slabs on which the Law was written (and the fragments of the first two). The people rejoiced and David himself forgot that he was king and danced in the street.

145

So all that God planned had happened. His people were settled and united in the land that he had given them, and David the king reigned in Jerusalem.

But David thought, I am king of Israel and I live in a palace. The God of Israel, king of the Universe, lives in a tent.

God knew what he was thinking and he chose a prophet named Nathan to take a message to David.

And God said to David: *You want to build me a beautiful house, don't you? David, I have lived in that tent since Moses brought the Law down from heaven and I came with it, and I have never complained. I have never asked anyone to build me a house and I am not starting now. You are a warrior; your work is to keep Israel safe. But I will allow your son to build me a house, and in return I shall make his family the royal house of this land.*

And knowing how much David wanted to build him a house, God let him buy the land where it would stand. And David bought also all the stone and iron and wood and brass to build the home of God.

And he said to his son Solomon, "God has promised me that when I die, you shall be king in my place, although you are not my eldest son. All my life I have fought the enemies of Israel, but now the kingdom is at peace, and God has promised that you shall reign in peace. I wanted to build him a house but he told me that I was a warrior and a shedder of blood, not a builder. Great buildings belong to peace time. You will build God's house, and our tribe, the house of Judah, will rule over Israel."

Now, in his lifetime David did many great and glorious things, and many brave deeds. But he did many wrong things too, and many foolish things. But he never forgot that God had made him king, and when he did wrong, God took care that Nathan the prophet told him what God thought. And always David was sorry for the wrongs he had done, and so God forgave him every time, and loved him to the end.

147

And David so loved his God that he hung his harp on the bedpost. When the wind blew across the strings at midnight, David would awake and light his lamp and study the Law till morning.

When David knew that he would soon die he called together all the great men of Israel and said to them, "God has chosen my son Solomon to be king after me, and he will build a great temple, a house for God, here in Jerusalem." And then, as God had told Moses how to make the box and the tent, the altar, the candlestick, and the mercy seat, David gave Solomon the blueprints for the temple and told him how to build it.

And before he died, David saw his son Solomon anointed king of Israel, and he died knowing that all God had promised was coming true. For God had said to Abraham: *Your children's children shall be a great nation.* And so they were. And a man of the tribe of Judah sat upon the throne.

Surely, now all would be well between God and his people?

Solomon and After

SOLOMON BEGAN WELL.

God came to him in a dream and said: *I am going to give you anything you ask for. What will you choose?*

Solomon thought, If I ask for great wealth he will give it to me; but if I ask for wisdom, everything else will come with it. And a wise man dies with a good name, which is the most valuable thing of all.

So Solomon asked for wisdom and his answer pleased God, who thought, Once again I have chosen well. The best of all David's sons is the king of the people of Israel. And he said to Solomon: *Because you have asked only to be wise, I will give you all the things that you did not ask for.*

Which was just what Solomon had reckoned.

And Solomon became famous for his wisdom, among his own people and throughout the world. But not all that he did was wise.

米

Still, he built the temple, a house for God, in Jerusalem. That is, he called men from all corners of the kingdom to build the house, and they had to leave their own work to do it. And so swiftly and so quietly was the stone cut and carried that people said that no man's hand had cut it. Solomon must have used the magical worm Shamir to cut the stones, and commanded angels to carry it to the city and set one block upon another. God and the workmen knew better.

And when the temple was finished, the box that Bezalel had made for Moses, where the

152

stones of the Law were kept, was brought into the temple. And after hundreds of years living in a tent, God at last had a house and could stretch out comfortably.

Then Solomon began to build a house for himself, as splendid as the house that he had built for God. It took seven years to build God's house. It was thirteen years before Solomon's house was finished.

And God said to Solomon: *I have heard your prayers and I am grateful for my house. Here will I live at the heart of Israel, as I promised your father, David, for as long as you and the people keep my Law and remember that I am the one God. For if you forget me, and forget my Law, and start to worship other gods, then I shall turn the people out of their land, out of my sight, and I shall destroy the temple.*

154

Perhaps Solomon did not believe that God would abandon the people he had chosen, and wreck his own house. Who knows? But he did not keep the Law of God and Moses.

For God and Moses had said, "If the people ever choose to have a king, he must not gather great wealth for himself; nor keep many horses; nor marry many wives."

But Solomon had great wealth, and he built barracks and stables for his army of horsemen and charioteers. And to keep the peace with neighboring kingdoms, he married many foreign princesses and built them each a palace.

And he let each wife worship her own foreign god, so that once again idols were set up in the land of Israel, and the people found it easier to worship gods that they could see, instead of their own God, who lived in the temple where no one could see him. How could they tell if he were there or not?

And it is said that on the night that Solomon married the daughter of Pharaoh Necho of Egypt, God sent the angel Gabriel down to plant a reed in the sea to the west of the land of Israel. And around that reed the silt settled, and land formed, and on the land there grew up a great city called Rome, from where armies came to conquer the people of Israel. Be that as it may, Solomon was not using the wisdom that God had given him, and God noticed.

And God noticed that although the kingdom of Israel was at peace with its neighbors, it was not at peace with itself. For the twelve tribes were still twelve tribes, not one, and each envied the others. A king of flesh and blood was not enough to hold the people together. Only God could do that, and now the people were worshipping idols again.

When Solomon died, his son Rehoboam came to the throne. He was weak and willful and not at all wise. So God chose a strong man called Jeroboam and made him leader of the northern tribes. And with Jeroboam, the chiefs of those tribes came to Rehoboam and tried to reason with him.

Rehoboam asked the advice of the men, who had served his father, Solomon. And they said, "Speak words of peace to the people of the north. Promise to deal fairly with them and they will be loyal."

But Rehoboam thought, What do these old men know? And he asked the advice of his own friends who had grown up with him, pampered and arrogant. And they said, "You are the king. There is none greater than you. Tell these rebels that you will crush them." And Rehoboam did as they said.

Now, the tribes of the north were Reuben, Simeon, Dan, Naphtali, and Gad; Asher, Issachar, Zebulun, Ephraim, and Manassah, all living in the lands that Joshua gave them when he led them out of the wilderness.

The tribes of the south were Judah and Benjamin.

And the ten tribes of the north said to Rehoboam, "We want nothing more to do with the house of David, the tribe of Judah." And they went back to their lands and called themselves the kingdom of Israel, and Jeroboam ruled over them.

All that was left in the south were two tribes, the kingdom of Judah, and Rehoboam ruled over them.

And Jeroboam made idols for the people to worship, to keep them from going south to the temple in Jerusalem.

That was the end of God's plan that his people should live as one nation and have no other gods but him. And he said to Jeroboam: *Was it for this that I made you leader of the northern tribes?*

Now, when God spoke to Abraham and Isaac and Jacob, he spoke as a father. He spoke as a friend to Moses, but now there seemed to be no point in speaking at all, for no matter what he said, the people of Israel and the people of Judah took little notice.

King followed king in the north; king followed king in the south. Some were bad, and some were worse, and a few were good, but the only way that God could speak to them now was through other people.

These were the men called prophets. God spoke to the prophets and showed them astonishing visions; and the prophets spoke to the kings and the people. And sometimes the people listened and sometimes they did not, for the two kingdoms fought each other, and they fought their neighbors, and all the while

159

the end of both kingdoms was coming, and no one saw it.

For far away in the east a great empire was growing: Assyria. And God spoke to the prophet Hosea and said: *Tell the people of Israel that unless they turn back from their evil ways I will send the Assyrians to conquer them.*

And in the south the prophet Isaiah saw a vision of God in the temple, surrounded by his great angels. And God said to Isaiah: *Tell the people of Judah that unless they turn back to me I will let the Assyrians conquer Jerusalem. They may make an alliance with Egypt, but that will not save them.*

Then prophet after prophet warned the peoples of Israel and Judah that unless they put their trust in God both kingdoms would fall to the enemy.

And so it was. For the Assyrians conquered the kingdom of the north and the people were driven away into exile and slavery.

Then God felt like a father whose son had gone to the bad, so he drove him away, saying: *It is his own fault that he has lost everything.*

But another great empire arose in the east: Babylon. And the armies of Babylon defeated the armies of Assyria, and Nebuchadnezzar, the king of Babylon, defeated the armies of Egypt and attacked Jerusalem, and the people of Judah were taken captive to Babylon.

161

Then God felt like a father whose second son went to the bad, and as he drove him away, he said to himself: *I have lost them both. It must be my fault for bringing them up so badly.*

Then the land that God had given to Abraham, where the children of Israel had lived for generations, was abandoned and left in ruins. The temple in Jerusalem was destroyed and God no longer had a place to live upon earth.

He returned to heaven and mourned with the angels for his lost people, and so great was his grief that the souls of the dead rose up and spoke.

Abraham cried, "Was it for this that you gave me a son in my old age?"

Isaac cried, "Was it for this that I lay bound on the altar to be sacrificed?"

Jacob cried, "Was it for this that I worked for Laban twenty years?"

Moses cried, "Was it for this that I led the people out of Egypt?"

Then Rachel, Jacob's wife, rose up and cried, "These are my children too. I let my sister be wed to the man I loved, instead of me, and did not speak out to shame her. How can you shame my children?"

And God said: *For your sake, Rachel, I will bring them back again.*

The Second Promise

NOT EVERYONE SUFFERED in exile.

Why, a girl called Esther, of the tribe of
Benjamin, became the wife of the king of Persia
himself, and saved her people from destruction.

But before that, when Nebuchadnezzar
besieged Jerusalem, he ordered four children of
the royal house of Judah to be taken to Babylon.
And they were brought up in the house of the
king, and taught to speak his language, and
given Babylonian names: Shadrach, Meshach,
Abednego, and Belteshazzar.

But among themselves they used their

true names, Hananiah, Mishael, Azariah, and
Daniel. And they remembered their true God,
the God of Israel, and they kept his Law.

And although they were far from home,
God remembered them and watched over them.
He gave them more wisdom than the king, could
teach them, and to Daniel he gave a special gift,
the same gift that he had given to Joseph, long
ago. Daniel could understand dreams. Then
God sent a message to the sleeping king, and
when Nebuchadnezzar awoke he called for his
wise men and said, "I have dreamed a dream and
I need to know what it means."

And the wise men said, "Oh, King, live
forever. Tell us the dream and we will tell you
what it means."

Nebuchadnezzar, in an evil mood, said,
"Unfortunately I have forgotten it, and if you
cannot tell me what it was I shall have you all
cut into small pieces."

When word went out of what the king
had threatened, Daniel came to him and said,
"Give me a little time and I will tell you what

you dreamed." Then he went home and prayed to God with Hananiah, Mishael, and Azariah that they would not be cut into small pieces with the rest of the wise men.

That night God sent Daniel the very same dream, and in the morning Daniel went to Nebuchadnezzar and said, "This is what your dream means. You are a great king, but the king

169

who comes after you will not be so great, and each king after that will be weaker than the last. And after all the kingdoms have fallen and passed away, God will set up a kingdom of his own, and that will last forever."

Then Nebuchadnezzar said to Daniel, "Your God must be the greatest of all gods," and he made Daniel a powerful man, to rule over the city. Daniel did not forget his friends Hananiah, Mishael, and Azariah, and the king also gave them great powers, but Daniel was the greatest.

Now, Nebuchadnezzar was impressed by the wonders that God could do, but all the same, he set up a giant idol of his own, and ordered the people to bow down before it. For he saw that God was great but he did not understand that he was the one God. And furthermore, he ordered that anyone who did not bow down to his idol should be flung into a burning fiery furnace.

So everyone bowed down before the idol

that Nebuchadnezzar the king had set up. But informers went to the king and said, "Those three young men from the west—the ones you put in power over the rest of us—are refusing to bow down in front of your idol."

So then the king was filled with rage, and he sent for Hananiah, Mishael, and Azariah, and when they stood before him, he said, "I understand that you refuse to bow down before my idol. Doubtless you have a god of your own. Will he save you when you are thrown into my burning fiery furnace?"

Hananiah, Mishael, and Azariah said, "Well, if he can, he will."

Then the king was seven times angrier than before and ordered the furnace to be stoked until it was seven times hotter. And while he watched, Hananiah, Mishael, and Azariah were flung into the furnace, which was now so hot that it burned up the men who flung them.

But God was watching, too. He turned to one of his great angels and said: *Go down.* And

171

there in the furnace, beside Hananiah, Mishael and Azariah, Nebuchadnezzar saw another man; and all four stood among the fiery flames unharmed, as if they stood in a shower of rain.

Then the king said, "In the future, anyone who speaks ill of the God of Israel will be cut into small pieces." And Nebuchadnezzar himself praised the God of Israel, so that when the prophet Jonah came to threaten him with God's anger, it was too late, and Jonah sulked for his wasted journey, much of it spent inside a large fish.

Daniel lived on at the king's court, but the king died at last and his heir, Belshazzar, sat upon the throne. Belshazzar had no respect for the God of Israel, and when he held a great feast the guests drank wine out of the golden cups and bowls that had been looted from the temple in Jerusalem.

And they raised the holy cups of unholy wine and drank toasts to the idols of Babylon. And while they were doing it, God leaned down and wrote something on the wall behind Belshazzar's head. He wrote these words:

MENE MENE TEKEL UPHARSEN

And no one knew what the words meant, but all were afraid, and Belshazzar was more afraid than any. And they sent for Daniel, the wisest of men, and asked him what the words meant.

So then Daniel said to Belshazzar, "Nebuchadnezzar learned that the God of Israel is one God. But you have despised my God; you drink wine from cups that were stolen from his own house. And now he has written you a letter, and this is what it says: you and your kingdom are finished and the Persians will take your throne and your land."

And that very night Belshazzar was killed, and the armies of Persia overran the kingdom of Babylon.

The king of Persia honored the God of Israel and Daniel lived to see some of his people return to Jerusalem and build a new, small temple.

But in its turn, the empire of Persia was overthrown by the empire of Greece, and after the Greeks came the Romans. The Romans allowed King Herod to build a new great temple, but he built not to the glory of God but to the glory of Herod, and in time the armies of Rome destroyed that temple in its turn.

The people of Israel were scattered over the face of the earth and never again did God speak to men or kings or prophets, or send down his angels. He had done all that he could; now he left them to get along as best they might, on their own, but they never lost hope.

For God had made them another promise, and they knew God kept his promises. He had promised to give them a land, and he had given it.

He had promised to take it away again, and he took it.

The new promise was this: that one day God would choose a leader from among the people and anoint him with oil, as Samuel had anointed David. And he would be called the Anointed One, the Messiah. And when the Messiah came, the troubles of the people would be over, for he would lead them against their enemies once and for all, and after that, the time of mankind in this world would be

177

done, and the people would be with God in the world to come.

No one knew who the Messiah would be, nor when he would arise, but there was nothing to be gained by sitting around and waiting, while empires rose and fell around them. As well as the promise, the people still had Torah, the Law, which told them how to live.

And for hundreds of years wise men debated and discussed how the laws should be kept, for times were always changing. But as long as the people lived by the Law they would know that they were still the people of the God of Israel, for this was the Law that God himself had given to Moses, to give to them, long ago when they fled from the land of Egypt, and an angel had gone before them like a tall cloud by day and a column of fire by night.

And the Messiah? Who knows?

Since those times other peoples have risen up and said, "These commandments are our commandments." "This Messiah is our Messiah." "This God is our God. There is only one way to worship him and that is our way. Everyone else is wrong."

And daily, people suffer and die because others think that their way is the wrong way. When the angels saw God making man and said, "No good will come of this," surely, they spoke the truth.

For some say there is no Messiah.

And some say that the Messiah has come already.

And some are still waiting.

Who is right? God knows.

Acknowledgments

In writing this book I have consulted:

The Book of God by Gabriel Josipovici (copyright © 1988, Yale University Press, New Haven and London)

Everyman's Talmud by Abraham Cohen (copyright © 1949, E. P. Dutton, New York; this edition published by Schocken Books, New York, 1975)

Humanism in Talmud and Midrash by Samuel Tobias Lachs (copyright © 1993, The Associated University Presses, London and Toronto)
J. M.

Special thanks are due to Ben Norland for his skill, sensitivity, and patience in helping me produce the illustrations.
D. P.